SELECTED PO

1930–1960

of

Vernon Watkins

by the same author

*

VERNON WATKINS

Selected Poems

1930-1960

FABER AND FABER

24 Russell Square

London

First published in this edition mcmlxvii
by Faber and Faber Limited
24 Russell Square, London W.C.1
Printed in Great Britain by
R. MacLehose and Company Limited
The University Press Glasgow

TO GWEN

Contents

Acknowledgment

Acknowledgment is made to *Wales, Life and Letters To-Day, The Listener, Horizon, Poetry (Chicago), Encounter, The London Magazine, The Nation* and *The Times Literary Supplement*, where many of these poems first appeared.

Discoveries

The poles are flying where the two eyes set:
America has not found Columbus yet.

Ptolemy's planets, playing fast and loose,
Foretell the wisdom of Copernicus.

Dante calls Primum Mobile, the First Cause:
'Love that moves the world and the other stars.'

Great Galileo, twisted by the rack,
Groans the bright sun from heaven, then breathes it back.

Blake, on the world alighting, holds the skies,
And all the stars shine down through human eyes.

Donne sees those stars, yet will not let them lie:
'We're tapers, too, and at our own cost die.'

The shroud-lamp catches. Lips are smiling there.
'Les flammes — déjà?' — The world dies, or Voltaire.

Swift, a cold mourner at his burial-rite,
Burns to the world's heart like a meteorite.

Beethoven deaf, in deafness hearing all,
Unwinds all music from sound's funeral.

Three prophets fall, the litter of one night:
Blind Milton gazes in fixed deeps of light.

Beggar of those Minute Particulars,
Yeats lights again the turmoil of the stars.

Motionless motion! Come, Tiresias,
The eternal flies, what's passing cannot pass.

'Solace in flight,' old Heraclitus cries;
Light changing to Von Hügel's butterflies.

Rilke bears all, thinks like a tree, believes,
Sinks in the hand that bears the falling leaves.

The stars! The signs! Great Angelo hurls them back.
His whirling ceiling draws the zodiac.

The pulse of Keats testing the axiom;
The second music when the sound is dumb.

The Christian Paradox, bringing its great reward
By loss; the moment known to Kierkegaard.

The Turning of the Leaves

Not yet! Do not yet touch,
Break not this branch of silver-birch,
Nor ask the stealthy river why it laves
Black roots that feed the leaves.

Ask first the flickering wren.
He will move further. Ask the rain.
No drop, though round, through that white miracle
Will sink, to be your oracle.

Not yet! Do not yet bend
Close to that root so tightly bound
Loosened by creeping waters as they run
Along the fork's rough groin.

Ask not the water yet
Why the root's tapering tendrils eat
Parched earth away that they may be
Nearer the source those fibres must obey.

Behind the bark your hands will find
No Sycorax or flying Daphne faned
And the brown ignorant water bindweed breeds
Not caring there what brows it braids.

Light in the branches weaves.
Hard is the waiting moment while it waves,
This tree whose trunk curves upward from the stream
Where faltering ripples strum.

See how it hangs in air.
The leaves are turning now. We cannot hear
The death and birth of life. But that disguise,
Look up now, softly: break it with your eyes.

The Collier

When I was born on Amman hill
A dark bird crossed the sun.
Sharp on the floor the shadow fell;
I was the youngest son.

And when I went to the County School
I worked in a shaft of light.
In the wood of the desk I cut my name:
Dai for Dynamite.

The tall black hills my brothers stood;
Their lessons all were done.
From the door of the school when I ran out
They frowned to watch me run.

The slow grey bells they rung a chime
Surly with grief or age.
Clever or clumsy, lad or lout,
All would look for a wage.

I learnt the valley flowers' names
And the rough bark knew my knees.
I brought home trout from the river
And spotted eggs from the trees.

A coloured coat I was given to wear
Where the lights of the rough land shone.
Still jealous of my favour
The tall black hills looked on.

They dipped my coat in the blood of a kid
And they cast me down a pit,
And although I crossed with strangers
There was no way up from it.

Soon as I went from the County School
I worked in a shaft. Said Jim,
'You will get your chain of gold, my lad,
But not for a likely time.'

And one said, 'Jack was not raised up
When the wind blew out the light
Though he interpreted their dreams
And guessed their fears by night.'

And Tom, he shivered his leper's lamp
For the stain that round him grew;
And I heard mouths pray in the after-damp
When the picks would not break through.

They changed words there in darkness
And still through my head they run,
And white on my limbs is the linen sheet
And gold on my neck the sun.

The Mummy

His eyes are closed. They are closed. His eyes are closed.
His hands are clenched. They are clenched. His hands are clenched.
The messenger comes. The letters are disciplined; they are disposed.
The black light quivers. Earth on Earth is avenged.

What has left music fast in the sockets of bone?
Had all been pattern, images sight had seen,
Blood would lie quiet, but something strokes the light, and a groan
Of great-rooted calm repels those images: nothing they mean.

Nothing here lives but the music in the eyes.
Hunting-scene, warriors, chariot, palm and wing
Bid the blood rest, thought perch where the time-bird sings or flies,
Year chasing year, following and following.

But tears wash these bones where parchments whisper to sand.
Here a laid vase offers the flying stream.
Sand darkening wakes a harp-string hidden, plucked by a blind
hand,
Crying this theme to the world, this world-surrounding theme:

Valiant, alive, his voice pursued the lands,
Ruled the white sea, held mountains in his keep.
Leave him with delicate instruments formed for delicate hands;
In this locked room of treasures let him who chose them sleep.

I lean down, crying: 'Touch me, lay hold on my Spring,
Reach up, for I have loosened, tearing your skies,
Fountains of light, ages of listening!'
But the bound hands are folded, the fold its word denies.

What shudder of music unfulfilled vibrates?
What draws to a dust-grain's fall most distant stars?

In the last taper's light what shadow meditates?
What single, athletic shape never cast on wall or vase?

What shudder of birth and death? What shakes me most?
Job his Maker answering, the Stricken exclaiming 'Rejoice!'
Gripping late in the shifting moment giant Earth, making Earth a
    ghost,
Who heard a great friend's death without a change of voice.

Elegy on the Heroine of Childhood

(IN MEMORY OF PEARL WHITE)

' . . . We died in you, and offered
Sweets to the Gods. . . .'

Who flung this world? What gangs proclaimed a truce,
Spinning the streets from bootlaces come loose?
What iron hoop in darkness slid
Chased by electric heels which hid
Cold faces behind pamphlets of the time?
Why was I left? What stairs had I to climb?

Four words catch hold. Dead exile, you would excite
In the red darkness, through the filtered light,
Our round, terrified eyes, when some
Demon of the rocks would come
And lock you in his house of moving walls:
You taught us first how loudly a pin falls.

From penny rows, when we began to spell,
We watched you, at the time when Arras fell,
Saw you, as in a death-ray seen,
Ride the real fear on a propped screen,
Where, through revolting brass, and darkness' bands,
Gaping, we groped with unawakened hands.

A sea-swung murmur, and a shout. Like shags
Under carved gods, with sweets in cone-shaped bags,
Tucked in to-morrow's unpaid fears,
Rucked there before the unguarded years,
We watched you, doomed, drowned, daggered, hurled from sight,
Fade from your clipped death in the tottering light.

Frantic, a blunted pattern showed you freed.
Week back to week I tread with nightmare speed,
Find the small entrance to large days,
Charging the chocolates from the trays,

14

Where, trailing or climbing the railing, we mobbed the dark
Of Pandemonium near Cwmdonkin Park.

Children return to mourn you. I retrace
Their steps to childhood's jealousies, a place
Of urchin hatred, shaken fists;
I drink the poison of the mists
To see you, a clear ghost before true day,
A girl, through wrestling clothes, caps flung in play.

From school's spiked railings, glass-topped, cat-walked walls,
From albums strewn, the streets' strange funerals,
We run to join the queue's coiled peel
Tapering, storming the Bastille,
Tumbling, with collars torn and scattered ties,
To thumbscrewed terror and the sea of eyes.

Night falls. The railing on which fast we pressed
Bears you, thumb-printed, to a death unguessed,
Before the time when you should rise
Venus to adolescent eyes,
A mermaid drying from your acid bath
Catching our lechery on a flying path.

Who has not seen the falling of a star?
Black liquorice made you bright before the War.
You glittered where the tongue was curled
Around the sweet fear of this world.
Doom's serial writing sprang upon the wall
Blind with a rush of light. We saw you fall.

How near, how far, how very faintly comes
Your tempest through a tambourine of crumbs,
Whose eye, by darkness sanctified,
Is brilliant with my boyhood's slide.
How silently at last the reel runs back
Through your three hundred deaths, now Death wears black.

Griefs of the Sea

It is fitting to mourn dead sailors,
To crown the sea with some wild wreath of foam
On some steep promontory, some cornercliff of Wales
Though the deaf wave hear nothing.

It is fitting to fling off clothing,
To enter the sea with plunge of seawreaths white
Broken by limbs that love the waters, fear the stars,
Though the blind wave grope under eyes that see, limbs that
     wonder,
Though the blind wave grope forward to the sand
With a greedy, silvered hand.

It is a horrible sound, the low wind's whistle
Across the seaweeds on the beach at night.
From stone to stone through hissing caves it passes
Up the curved cliff and shakes the prickly thistle
And spreads its hatred through the grasses.

In spite of that wicked sound
Of the wind that follows us like a scenting hound,
It is fitting on the curved cliff to remember the drowned,
To imagine them clearly for whom the sea no longer cares,
To deny the language of the thistle, to meet their foot-firm tread
Across the dark-sown tares
Who were skilful and erect, magnificent types of godhead,
To resist the dogging wind, to accuse the sea-god;
Yet in that gesture of anger we must admit
We were quarrelling with a phantom unawares.

For the sea turns whose every drop is counted
And the sand turns whose every grain a holy hour-glass holds
And the weeds turn beneath the sea, the sifted life slips free,
And the wave turns surrendering from its folds
All things that are not sea, and thrown off is the spirit
By the sea, the riderless horse which they once mounted.

Yeats in Dublin

(IN MEMORY OF W. B. YEATS)

A rich lupin-garden,
A long, amber room,
A bronze head, bookshelves
Glittering in that gloom;
And threads, threads, threads of the sea,
Threads of the birds of doom.

Impression of rain-wet, moving leaves.
A dog upon the drive
Casts a questioning shadow
Where secret flowers connive.
A terrible seabird. Folded wings.
Then the gannet's dive.

'From such a treadle of the sea
Your foot may never come,
Never without breaking
The pattern of the loom:
All the ages go to make
The thread around your thumb.'

'O come back,' the seabirds cry,
'To the raindrops' hammerings,
Down to the ignorant Irish sea
Crossed by encircling wings;
Under the sea dumb grains, great rocks:
Think of these old things.'

But Yeats, Yeats the poet
Under Dublin skies,
After the ten years' journey
On which no seagull flies,
After the waves of silence
I look him in the eyes.

Fresh from the shining sunlight
We came on his dark seat,
Shook hands, paused, were dumb there
Fearing to tire him out,
Though his raised head was noble,
His voice firm and sweet.

'Tell me about that young group
Of Welsh writers,' he said,
'Whose poems in that paper you sent me
The other day I read.'
An image stands on Carmarthen sands
With the black birds overhead.

'The young poets,' he murmured,
'Toil too much. They lay
Something on their table,
And dissect, and wear it away
Till nothing but the grit is left;
But all song is gay.

There must always be a quality
Of nonchalance in the work.
The intellect is impotent
Labouring in the dark,
For a poem is always
A piece of luck.

Who can foretell the run of luck
Or where the luck may fall?
Watching the roulette-wheel
We see the spinning ball,
But where it stops and comes to rest
The place is magical.

The Psychical Research Society
Lately has found

It can experimentally
Foresee that resting-ground
A second before the fall of space
And the death of sound.

Much the treasure-hoarding mind
Values its sum,
But to a breath's vibration
All is held there dumb;
All is reduced to nothing;
Then the luck will come.

Against blinding darkness
A man's blood is thrown,
Striving for that intensity
Which danced before time ran;
That thing, for lack of a better name,
I call 'Eternal Man'.

A poet seeks his deepest thought,
Then finds, when it is made,
A loyalty has held it,
Not by time betrayed,
The very distance measured
By the blood's shade.

In an early poem I set myself
The task to unite
The myths of all ages
In a single night,
To draw their tale, not on the wall
But in the tip of the light.

I might have made it with the myths
Of Ireland alone,

But somewhere in my mind's eye
I saw Priam's throne.
Usna I wanted, but Troy too,
So I put Troy down.'

'Did the idea come slowly,'
I questioned, 'did it unfold
At once, or from the leaves themselves
As from a sculptor's mould?
Was it your mind that saw the words,
Or was your mind told?'

'I made it,' with a slow smile
Said that Irishman,
'Looking at a lady's photograph
Where all those myths began;
So naturally it came slowly.'
And he went on:

'A critic who has pleased me
(Though the best attack)
Says that the style is public
In my latest work;
That near to my youth, with a difference,
Song is going back.

That difference is important
In poem or in play.
Hard as thoughts in the bone to find
Are naked words to say;
Write, get rid of rhetoric;
Cut the dead wood away.

Cast off poetic diction first
And find what is your own.
Learn what reason could not teach
From the marrow in the bone.

Reject false decoration
And make the whole work one.

To-day I summon boyhood's reed
But bid that same reed break,
For broken things are powerful
Being bruised and trampled. Blake
And Burns had a public style;
But others found a fake,

The trick and slang of a slippery speech
Trite and second-hand;
Pandering to the popular ear
They did not understand
That truth must cut harder
Than the diamond.'

I asked, had he stirred enmity.
'Yes, my work was banned.
It was the laymen squeaked and squealed
And would not let it stand,
Never the hand of blessing,
Always the felon's hand.

But before my book 'A Vision' appeared
The Bishops began to urge
A ban on its publication
Fearing its views at large;
Then they heard it was a guinea,
And they dropped the charge.

'The Resurrection' would not have been played
But for a general strike.
Men who insist on vessels
Dare not see them break,

Terrified should the dead walk
Or the sleeper wake.

I met, in America,
A holy man who said:
'There will always be miracle —
(He raised his old, white head)
There will always be revelation,'
That old saint said.

A saint. I met his follower then.
He professed belief in all
The tenets of the Church's creed,
Mass and ritual,
Except the immortality
Of the human soul.

Another priest I asked which road
To salvation lay.
'Go to Mass, go to Mass,'
Was all that priest would say.
'It will take just twenty minutes.
Go, and you need not pray.'

Then, when I put a question
In salvation's track,
'Read what you like,' the priest replied,
'A great or a holy book.
I take when I go praying
A Dante bound in black.'

Yeats justified the parish priest,
One that could curse and bless,
Especially curse, and blame bad crops
On the peasants' wickedness.
'They must have their magician:
He is neither more nor less.'

We from two countries coming
Took tea, and talked of Synge's
Islands, behind us sunlight
And the path of wings,
Before us thought and images
Beaten into rings.

Thought, grief-impassioned, drifted
To Coole, and Lady Gregory:
'Have the trees grown a little
Around Thoor Ballylee?'
One by one he raised those names
Between the waves of the sea.

Lionel Johnson, Dowson,
And political men betrayed,
Murdered by their excess of love
Or by a dream they made;
Synge's mighty statements;
The brightness of the shade.

'We have the folk in Ireland;
The English make it up.
How can a country's language thrive
If an abstract shape
Battening on the vigorous man
Sucks the blood-drop?

When I first went to London
I was looking for a technique.
I had the folk behind me,
My food was there to seek,
But without the subtlety London taught
I could not learn to speak.

I got technique from a man who was
A very bad poet indeed.
He taught me to appreciate
The small stops of the reed;
The Minutiae of a poem
He first made me heed.

What if the labour all seem vain,
What if years are spent
Chiselling and chiselling
The stubborn element?
All is rewarded on a breath
By an accident.

My quarrel with those Londoners
Is that they try
To substitute psychology
For the naked sky
Of metaphysical movement,
And drain the blood dry.

All is materialism, all
The catchwords they strew,
Alien to the blood of man. — '
One ranting slogan drew
That 'Poetry must have news in it':
'The reverse is true.'

I questioned him: 'How can there be
A national poetry?
What can we make or what resist
When all is like the sea?'
He said: 'You must resist the stream
Of mechanical apathy.'

Speaking of leaders, he affirmed,
'The best is he who knows
The fancy-dress of politics
From his garden-clothes,
Who understands the popular mask,
Those deceiving shows.'

He spoke of de Valera,
A charming, cultured man
Who found upon the platform
True culture under ban,
Then uttered out of vehemence
Words he would say to none.

We talked of national movements.
He pondered the chance
Of Welshmen reviving
The fire of song and dance,
Driving a lifeless hymnal
From that inheritance.

I thought of rough mountains,
The poverty of the heath.
'Though leaders sway the crowd,' I said,
'Power is underneath.
The sword of Taliesin
Would never fit a sheath.'

'The leaders and the poets
Are not in unison.
When Hitler struck a medal
He knew that George* won,
But he had not served his movement,
So qualified for none.'

* Stefan George (1868–1933)

He questioned my French friend,
And his words remain
Shining like pebbles
Under the flow of the Seine,
Where Synge had walked with him,
Where he had met Verlaine.

The work of Péguy he had known,
Claudel and Valéry,
The sacred tapestry of Joan
And Christian charity,
Mallarmé's pupil's masterpiece,
The Graveyard by the Sea.

Spirits whirling about us
Were laid by a look,
Ghosts turned in delicate light
To gold on the edge of a book,
Wound in the shroud of a still page
Which no man took.

Light in the drawing-room,
Daylight on the lawn,
Book-shadows in the corners
Seemed to have drawn
Spirits from the back of the mind,
From conception's dawn.

Yeats and his wife once more
Asked of the Tower
Where I had stood last year
A dumb, low-breathed hour,
Watching the blade of the grass
And the grass-flower.

Then, as the heron
Rises from the stream,
He raised from the haunted chair
His tall, proud frame
In that dazzling background
Of heroic dream.

Now, as a child sees
Daybreak on a wall,
His image showed me in a flash
Birth and burial,
The trouble of the lovely song,
Parnell's Funeral.

'I must work' and 'I must rest'
In one breath he said,
Unconsciously, a blind man
By a blind hand led,
All creation hanging
On that double thread.

My friend and I were silent
Witnessing that thing
Which of the sacred rivers
Had touched the secret spring
Making, in the youth of age,
The dumb stone sing.

With visionary footsteps
Slow, he crossed the room,
He who had made the dead lips sing
And celebrate love in doom,
About him the sages
Of Byzantium.

To that broken vision
What could we bring,
Blinded by the shadow

Standing in sheaves. Which way would I do you wrong?
Low, crumbling doorway of the infirm to the mansions of evening,
And poor, shrunken furrow where the potatoes are sown,
I shall not unnumber one soul I have stood with and known
To regain your stars struck by horses, your sons of God breaking
    in song.

Note: Goleufryn (Welsh, 'golen', light, and 'fryn', hill) is pronounced 'Go-live-rin', with 'live' here rhyming with 'dive'.

Foal

Darkness is not dark, nor sunlight the light of the sun
But a double journey of insistent silver hooves.
Light wakes in the foal's blind eyes as lightning illuminates corn
With a rustle of fine-eared grass, where a starling shivers.

And whoever watches a foal sees two images,
Delicate, circling, born, the spirit with blind eyes leaping
And the left spirit, vanished, yet here, the vessel of ages
Clay-cold, blue, laid low by her great wide belly the hill.

See him break that circle, stooping to drink, to suck
His mother, vaulted with a beautiful hero's back
Arched under the singing mane,
Shaped to her shining, pricked into awareness
By the swinging dug, amazed by the movement of suns;
His blue fellow has run again down into grass,
And he slips from that mother to the boundless horizons of air,
Looking for that other, the foal no longer there.

But perhaps
In the darkness under the tufted thyme and downtrodden winds,
In the darkness under the violet's roots, in the darkness of the
     pitcher's music,
In the uttermost darkness of a vase
There is still the print of fingers, the shadow of waters.
And under the dry, curled parchment of the soil there is always a
     little foal
Asleep.

So the whole morning he runs here, fulfilling the track
Of so many suns; vanishing the mole's way, moving
Into mole's mysteries under the zodiac,
Racing, stopping in the circle. Startled he stands
Dazzled, where darkness is green, where the sunlight is black,
While his mother, grazing, is moving away
From the lagging star of those stars, the unrisen wonder
In the path of the dead, fallen from the sun in her hooves,
And eluding the dead hands, begging him to play.

31

Ophelia

Stunned in the stone light, laid among the lilies,
Still in the green wave, graven in the reed-bed,
Lip-read by clouds in the language of the shallows,
Lie there, reflected.

Soft come the eddies, cold between your fingers.
Rippling through cresses, willow-trunk and reed-root,
Gropes the grey water; there the resting mayfly
Burns like an emerald.

Haunting the path, Laertes falls to Hamlet;
He, the young Dane, the mover of your mountains,
Sees the locked lids, your nunnery of sorrows,
Drowned in oblivion.

Silvered with dawn, the pattern of the bridge-vault
Dancing, a light-skein woven by the stream there,
Travels through shade the story of your dying,
Sweet-named Ophelia.

Dense was your last night, thick with stars unnumbered.
Bruised, the reeds parted. Under them the mud slipped,
Yielding. Scuttling and terrified, the moorhen
Left you to sink there.

Few, faint the petals carried on the surface,
Watched by those bright eyes ambushed under shadow,
Mouse, bird and insect, bore you witness, keeping
Pace ever silent.

Here, then, you lingered, late upon the world's rim,
Matched here the princelike, stopped, and were confounded,
Finding that image altered in the water's
Bitter remembrance.

Passion recalls the tumult of your story,
Midnight revives it, where your name is printed;
Yet from the water, intimate, there echoes:
'Tell this to no man'.

Bride-veils of mist fall, brilliant are the sunbeams,
Open the great leaves, all the birds are singing.
Still unawake in purity of darkness
Whiter than daylight

Dream the soft lids, the white, the deathly sleeping;
Closed are the lashes: day is there a legend.
Rise from the fair flesh, from the midnight water,
Child too soon buried.

The Healing of the Leper

O, have you seen the leper healed,
And fixed your eyes upon his look?
There is the book of God revealed,
And God has made no other book.

The withered hand which time interred
Grasps in a moment the unseen.
The word we had not heard, is heard.
What we are then, we had not been.

Plotinus, preaching on heaven's floor,
Could not give praise like that loud cry
Bursting the bondage of death's door;
For we die once; indeed we die.

What Sandro Botticelli found
Rose from the river where we bathe:
Music the air, the stream, the ground;
Music the dove, the rock, the faith:

And all that music whirled upon
The eyes' deep-sighted, burning rays,
Where all the prayers of labours done
Are resurrected into praise.

But look: his face is like a mask
Surrounded by the beat of wings.
Because he knows that ancient task
His true transfiguration springs.

All fires the prophets' words contained
Fly to those eyes, transfixed above.
Their awful precept has remained:
'Be nothing, first; and then, be love'.

The Song of the Good Samaritan

I sing of the Good Samaritan, of
Pity and the Fixed Stars. Him the Awakeners bless
Who heal the Earth with silent tumult of love.

There came the configuration of ages, less
Than his moment of deepest shadow. I sing of his
Leap into God, of the trial of gentleness.

Night. Death. And forever the distances
Woven by the pulse, that infinite loom of heaven;
Then out of the water a kiss, a leper's kiss,

Given through the dark. Look up! The moment is given
To the dog derided and scorned; and a look outpaces
The beautiful horses mythology thought to have driven.

Look. Look up! Frozen light! The Gorgon grimaces
Of the stone-blind heaven freeze blood in the marvelling child
Standing alone on the bed near the strange toy-faces.

Constellations! Look! The Fixed Stars! Blind meteors whirled!
Night's pattern, the clustered myths! On the Milky Road
Towards milk-white Jericho stumbles one from the world

Leading a mule, borne down with its dusty load,
To the shade of a tree, to a trough. The mythologies shrink,
And the nameless image is healed of its murderous goad.

Font of the fingers, water where asses drink,
Winged horses above you scattering, manes of the Norn,
And heroic Pegasus, leap into light from the brink.

Swallows quiver, rounding the magical horn
Of fullness, emptied for John's wild honey. They break
Light with their wings, and the era of love is born.

He broke the classical falsehood, summoned awake
A world from dust with the secret worlds of his tears.
Shut in those heavens he heard the mythologies shake.

Their violent haunches taut, their delicate ears
Coiled to a point, a horn growing out of each head,
They know they are crystal, their breath the smoke of the spheres.

Centaurs, unicorns, wondering, weaving a thread
From the loom of silence, coiling all ages at once
To a hero's masterful, measured, arrogant tread.

And music sprung from the rock, from the pagan dance
Of firelit bodies, heard in the cataract's head;
A prince of warriors, Venus guiding his lance.

Those heroes gather the spaces through which they have sped
To ivory silence or toil of intractable bronze,
Resurrecting the ravisher's cup, the wine of the dead.

Yet the buried see them as the unforgiving, spun
From cruelty's frenzy back through a minotaur maze,
A battle of Centaurs fled into the blaze of suns;

Fled, fled, in a furious pattern of praise
From the throat of light, a thunder of galloping feet
Riding the rim that acclaims their arrogant days.

What vision startled a prophet in that hard heat
Of the wayside's ultimate shadow? He bent to hear
The spheres from a donkey suffer their proud retreat.

Then, as he looked on those features, sphere upon sphere
Shone round the loom of the hand. No name had this
That buried and raised all time in the spring of a tear.

And he heard through heaven the retreating distances,
Timbrels, the long gold trumpet, the Pharaoh's car,
Heroic song, gold idols, the pagan dances.

Even as a child I began to say: How far?
Parting the curtain, the winding-sheet of the dead.
The loom of the hand has the pathway of every star.

Disappearance of the proud horses! Circling in dread,
Stampeding in light, he heard the mythologies shrink,
The rushing stars, their reverberant, thundering tread;

From a little worn-away trough where asses drink,
One by one, and above them, finding the sea,
Swallows pass, and their world ripples over the brink.

'O moment,' he breathed, 'frail as the branch of a tree,
This act is secret, eluding all fabulous joys.
The wound I suffer, the joy I am bearing, is he.

For they were movement itself, but mine was a choice
Between those visions acclaimed by pride overthrown,
And the downcast, intimate eyes, the source of the voice.

Dip, swallows. The Centaurs already are stone,
And the water listens, finding continually crooked
The path the asses have paced, the thread you have flown.

Now, if I speak, my words can belong to no book
For my fingers mingle the language of water and dove,
Ending, here at the source, the journey they took.

Out of the dust I raised this image of love.
Moment of darkness, moment, still you are mine,
Though the proud-winged, galloping horses disdainfully move

From the wounded god, the arena of dust and sand.

And only the tilted loom is lucky, divine,
Where the mocked, unpremeditated bowl of the hand
Makes the world nothing, pouring in oil and wine.'

The Feather

I stoop to gather a seabird's feather
Fallen on the beach,
Torn from a beautiful drifting wing;
What can I learn or teach,
Running my finger through the comb
And along the horny quill?
The body it was torn from
Gave out a cry so shrill,
Sailors looked from their white road
To see what help was there.
It dragged the winds to a drop of blood
Falling through drowned air,
Dropping from the sea-hawk's beak,
From frenzied talons sharp;
Now if the words they lost I speak
It must be to that harp
Under the strange, light-headed sea
That bears a straw of the nest.
Unless I make that melody,
How can the dead have rest?

Sheer from wide air to the wilderness
The victim fell, and lay;
The starlike bone is fathomless,
Lost among wind and spray.
This lonely, isolated thing
Trembles amid their sound.
I set my finger on the string
That spins the ages round.
But let it sleep, let it sleep
Where shell and stone are cast;
Its ecstasy the Furies keep,
For nothing here is past.

The perfect into night must fly;
On this the winds agree.
How could a blind rock satisfy
The hungers of the sea?

Gravestones

Look down. The dead have life.
Their dreadful night accompanies our Springs.
Touch the next leaf:
Such darkness lives there, where a last grief sings.

Light blinds the whirling graves.
Lost under rainwet earth the letters run.
A finger grieves,
Touching worn names, bearing daughter and son.

Here the quick life was borne,
A fountain quenched, fountains with sufferings crowned.
Creeds of the bone
Summoned from darkness what no Sibyl found.

Truly the meek are blest
Past proud men's trumpets, for they stilled their fame
Till this late blast
Gave them their muted, and their truest name.

Sunk are the stones, green-dewed,
Blunted with age, touched by cool, listening grass.
Vainly these died,
Did not miraculous silence come to pass.

Yet they have lovers' ends,
Lose to hold fast, as violets root in frost.
With stronger hands
I see them rise through all that they have lost.

I take a sunflower down,
With light's first faith persuaded and entwined.
Break, buried dawn,
For the dead live, and I am of their kind.

The Lady with the Unicorn

About this lady many fruitful trees.
There the chaste unicorn before her knees
Stares in a glass to purify her sight.
At her right hand a lion sits,
And through the foliage, in and out, there flits
Many a bird; then hounds, with deer in flight:
Light is her element; her tapestry is light.

There is her mediaeval music met.
On the high table-top, with damask set
To charm, between the chaste beast and the strong,
An organ which her fingers play
Rests, and her pretty servant's hands obey
Those pipes with bellows to sustain their song
Attuned to distant stars, making their short life long.

This ended, gathered from some leafy way,
That servant brings her flowers upon a tray.
She lifts them to inhale their magic breath.
Caught in that breath's elusive maze,
She marvels. On a stool a monkey plays
With flowers from wicker trailing, strewn beneath,
A heaven of fragrance breathing through their mask of death.

Next, her right hand upholds that coat-of-arms
Seeming love's guardian against war's alarms,
And with her left she grips the upright horn.
This touch, while birds through branches peer,
Consecrates all the beasts as they appear,
Frisking among dark foliage to adorn
Her fingers that caress the constant unicorn.

A lion rampant grips the upright pole.
Her serving-maid now proffers her a bowl
Of peaches, damsons, almonds, grapes, and sweets.

If there is white, or has been white, it must have been
When His eyes looked down and made the leper clean.
White will not be, apart, though the trees try
Spirals of blossom, their green conspiracy.
She who touched His garment saw no white tree.

Lovers speak of Venus, and the white doves,
Jubilant, the white girl, myth's whiteness, Jove's,
Of Leda, the swan, whitest of his loves.
Lust imagines him, web-footed Jupiter, great down
Of thundering light; love's yearning pulls him down
On the white swan-breast, the magical lawn,
Involved in plumage, mastered by the veins of dawn.

In the churchyard the yew is neither green nor black.
I know nothing of Earth or colour until I know I lack
Original white, by which the ravishing bird looks wan.
The mound of dust is nearer, white of mute dust that dies
In the soundfall's great light, the music in the eyes,
Transfiguring whiteness into shadows gone,
Utterly secret. I know you, black swan.

Music of Colours:
The Blossom Scattered

O, but how white is white, white from shadows come,
Sailing white of clouds, not seen before
On any snowfield, any shore;
Or this dense blue, delivered from the tomb,
White of the risen body, fiery blue of sky,
Light the saints teach us, light we learn to adore;
Not space revealed it, but the needle's eye
Love's dark thread holding, when we began to die.
It was the leper's, not the bird's cry,
Gave back that glory, made that glory more.

I cannot sound the nature of that spray
Lifted on wind, the blossoms falling away,
A death, a birth, an earthy mystery,
As though each petal stirring held the whole tree
That grew, created on the Lord's day.
There is no falling now. Yet for time's sake
These blossoms are scattered. They fall. How still they are.
They drop, they vanish, where all blossoms break.
Who touches one dead blossom touches every star.

So the green Earth is first no colour and then green.
Spirits who walk, who know
All is untouchable, and, knowing this, touch so,
Who know the music by which white is seen,
See the world's colours in flashes come and go.
The marguerite's petal is white, is wet with rain,
Is white, then loses white, and then is white again
Not from time's course, but from the living spring,
Miraculous whiteness, a petal, a wing,
Like light, like lightning, soft thunder, white as jet,
Ageing on ageless breaths. The ages are not yet.

Is there a tree, a bud, that knows not this:
White breaks from darkness, breaks from such a kiss
No mind can measure? Locked in the branching knot,
Conception shudders; that interior shade
Makes light in darkness, light where light was not;
Then the white petal, of whitest darkness made,
Breaks, and is silent. Immaculate they break,
Consuming vision, blinding eyes awake,
Dazzling the eyes with music, light's unspoken sound,
White born of bride and bridegroom, when they take
Love's path through Hades, engendered of dark ground.

Leda remembers. The rush of wings cast wide.
Sheer lightning, godhead, descending on the flood.
Night, the late, hidden waters on the moon's dark side.
Her virgin secrecy, doomed against time to run.
Morning. The visitation. All colours hurled in one.
Struggling with night, with radiance! That smothering glory cried:
'Heavenborn am I. White-plumaged heart, you beat against the
      sun!'
All recollection sinking from the dazzled blood.

She woke, and her awakened wings were fire,
Darkened with light; O blinding white was she
With white's bewildering darkness. So that secret choir
Know, in the thicket, and witness more than we,
Listening to early day, dew's voice, the lightest feet,
As though Saint Francis passing, told who they were,
Fledged of pure spirit, though upheld by air.
I think one living is already there,
So sound asleep she is, her breath so faint,
She knows, she welcomes the footstep of the saint,
So still, so moving, joy sprung of despair,
And the two feasts, where light and darkness meet.

The Turning of the Stars

There is a moment when Apollo's tree
Is Daphne still. The Past is not the Past
But wound within a ring
So finely wrought,
It knows each path and avenue of thought.
Downward he looks, through heaven and earth, to see
The sunlight and dayspring
Caught in her eyes, all uttered love surpassed
By that first heaven which knows her timelessly.

There is a touch, before the wall of bark
Echoes the music of those timeless hands,
The pivot of the god
Like light revealed
Where all the stars seem fallen in one field,
And secret, where the underleaf is dark,
Language is understood
Green as a spring, translated for all lands,
A touch to which rivers of leaves must hark.

Look. In the midnight heaven two stars draw near,
First the awakening laurel pressed by lips,
Her mortal destiny,
Her walk, her grief,
Then her ascending star of true belief;
Opposed, of differing glories, they appear,
Each on its axle-tree
Whirling, two heavenly bodies, to eclipse,
Pitched into darkness by love's greater year.

Miraculous, the flight of measured thought
Crosses the rebel fire of burning youth;
A choir of tranquil heads
Moving sublime
Through Raphael's heaven, from distance into time,

Inspired the pupil Perugino taught
To paint heaven's periods,
His mind being in its silence fixed on truth:
Unrest in calm, calm in unrest he sought.

Galileo, spun, recanting, to the stars,
Through the smoked glass of time presumed to watch
With monstrous emphasis
The disc of light
Edged by the rim of that great wheel in flight;
Copernicus proclaimed, we turned like Mars;
He checked the sun by this.
Alighieri, fixed yet flying, knelt to match
The speed of distance to the burial-vase.

Circle on circle, purgatorial years
Whirl against time the union of the blest.
A man may bind the stars
To his own bent
By faith protected, till that grave ascent
Find a new pivot for the moving spheres;
Or this may come to pass:
One intense moment may consume the rest,
A flash translate blind mortals into seers.

So love descends: the star which blots out heaven
Moves in the morning of our making hands.
Where Raphael's heavens project
On Mary's dread
The Infant Christ, a halo round His head,
He seems, the firstfruits of their sleep, to have given
To living intellect
The life of faith their death in faith demands;
His broken bread affirmed the sleepers' leaven.

About us garlands of earth's natural green
Quicken with may and hide the blackbird's clutch.
Leaves cover up the well,

And buds begin
To break, and hide the fountain's origin.
Spring behind Spring, star behind star, unseen,
Revolve in seed and cell.
Vision fulfils the source of visible touch.
Invisible dancers make our feet serene.

There is a power that holds me by a chain,
So ancient is the love that guards this book,
Inscrutable that praise;
I see the crash,
Fleece and spent fury, Sodom's deluge-flash;
I see the wide world sink, and rise again,
Hung in pure night, ablaze
With million worlds united in a look
Where boundless glory astounds the eye of the brain.

Verse is a part of silence. I have known
Always that declamation is impure.
This language best fits prayer,
The crystal night
Teeming with worlds in mathematic height.
Prodigious darkness guards its undertone,
And though that wheel of air
Seems to leave nothing earthly to endure,
The likeness, not the original, is gone.

Taliesin in Gower

Late I return, O violent, colossal, reverberant, eavesdropping sea.
My country is here. I am foal and violet. Hawthorn breaks from my
  hands.
I watch the inquisitive cormorant pry from the praying rock of
  Pwlldu,
Then skim to the gulls' white colony, to Oxwich's cockle-strewn
  sands.

I have seen the curlew's triangular print, I know every inch of his
  way.
I have gone through the door of the foundered ship, I have slept in
  the winch of the cave
With pine-log and unicorn-spiral shell secreting the colours of day;
I have been taught the script of the stones, and I know the tongue of
  the wave.

I witness here in a vision the landscape to which I was born,
Three smouldering bushes of willow, like trees of fire, and the
  course
Of the river under the stones of death, carrying the ear of corn
Withdrawn from the moon-dead chaos of rocks overlooking its
  secret force.

I see, a marvel in Winter's marshes, the iris break from its sheath
And the dripping branch in the ache of sunrise frost and shadow
  redeem
With wonder of patient, living leaf, while Winter, season of death,
Rebukes the sun, and grinds out men's groans in the voice of its
  underground stream.

Yet now my task is to weigh the rocks on the level wings of a bird,
To relate these undulations of time to a kestrel's motionless poise.
I speak, and the soft-running hour-glass answers; the core of the
  rock is a third:
Landscape survives, and these holy creatures proclaim their
  regenerate joys.

I know this mighty theatre, my footsole knows it for mine.
I am nearer the rising pewit's call than the shiver of her own wing.
I ascend in the loud waves' thunder, I am under the last of the nine.
In a hundred dramatic shapes I perish, in the last I live and sing.

All that I see with my sea-changed eyes is a vision too great for the
    brain.
The luminous country of auk and eagle rocks and shivers to earth.
In the hunter's quarry this landscape died; my vision restores it
    again.
These stones are prayers; every boulder is hung on a breath's
    miraculous birth.

Gorse breaks on the steep cliff-side, clings earth, in patches
    blackened for sheep,
For grazing fired; now the fair weather comes to the ravens'
    pinnacled knoll.
Larks break heaven from the thyme-breathing turf; far under,
    flying through sleep,
Their black fins cutting the rainbow surf, the porpoises follow the
    shoal.

They are gone where the river runs out, there where the breakers
    divide
The lacework of Three Cliffs Bay in a music of two seas;
A heron flaps where the sandbank holds a dyke to the twofold tide,
A wave-encircled isthmus of sound which the white bird-
    parliament flees.

Rhinoceros, bear and reindeer haunt the crawling glaciers of age
Beheld in the eye of the rock, where a javelin'd arm held stiff,
Withdrawn from the vision of flying colours, reveals, like script on
    a page,
The unpassing moment's arrested glory, a life locked fast in the cliff.

Now let the great rock turn. I am safe with an ear of corn,
A repository of light once plucked, from all men hidden away.
I have passed through a million changes. In a butterfly coracle
    borne,
My faith surmounting the Titan, I greet the prodigious bay.

I celebrate you, marvellous forms. But first I must cut the wood,
Exactly measure the strings, to make manifest what shall be.
All Earth being weighed by an ear of corn, all heaven by a drop of
    blood.
How shall I loosen this music to the listening, eavesdropping sea?

   Note: Pwlldu (Welsh for 'black pool') is pronounced 'Poollh-
dee'.

The Heron

The cloud-backed heron will not move:
He stares into the stream.
He stands unfaltering while the gulls
And oyster-catchers scream.
He does not hear, he cannot see
The great white horses of the sea,
But fixes eyes on stillness
Below their flying team.

How long will he remain, how long
Have the grey woods been green?
The sky and the reflected sky,
Their glass he has not seen,
But silent as a speck of sand
Interpreting the sea and land,
His fall pulls down the fabric
Of all that windy scene.

Sailing with clouds and woods behind,
Pausing in leisured flight,
He stepped, alighting on a stone,
Dropped from the stars of night.
He stood there unconcerned with day,
Deaf to the tumult of the bay,
Watching a stone in water,
A fish's hidden light.

Sharp rocks drive back the breaking waves,
Confusing sea with air.
Bundles of spray blown mountain-high
Have left the shingle bare.
A shipwrecked anchor wedged by rocks,
Loosed by the thundering equinox,
Divides the herded waters,
The stallion and his mare.

Yet no distraction breaks the watch
Of that time-killing bird.
He stands unmoving on the stone;
Since dawn he has not stirred.
Calamity about him cries,
But he has fixed his golden eyes
On water's crooked tablet,
On light's reflected word.

Taliesin and the Spring of Vision

'I tread the sand at the sea's edge, sand of the hour-glass,
And the sand receives my footprint, singing:
"You are my nearmost, you who have travelled the farthest,
And you are my constant, who have endured all vicissitudes
In the cradle of sea, Fate's hands, and the spinning waters.
The measure of past grief is the measure of present joy.
Your tears, which have dried to Chance, now spring from a secret.
Here time's glass breaks, and the world is transfigured in music." '

So sang the grains of sand, and while they whirled to a pattern
Taliesin took refuge under the unfledged rock.
He could not see in the cave, but groped with his hand,
And the rock he touched was the socket of all men's eyes,
And he touched the spring of vision. He had the mind of a fish
That moment. He knew the glitter of scale and fin.
He touched the pin of pivotal space, and he saw
One sandgrain balance the ages' cumulus cloud.

Earth's shadow hung. Taliesin said: 'The penumbra of history is
    terrible.
Life changes, breaks, scatters. There is no sheet-anchor.
Time reigns; yet the kingdom of love is every moment,
Whose citizens do not age in each other's eyes.
In a time of darkness the pattern of life is restored
By men who make all transience seem an illusion
Through inward acts, acts corresponding to music.
Their works of love leave words that do not end in the heart.'

He still held rock. Then three drops fell on his fingers,
And Future and Past converged in a lightning flash:
'It was we who instructed Shakespeare, who fell upon Dante's eyes,
Who opened to Blake the Minute Particulars. We are the soul's
    rebirth.'

Taliesin answered: 'I have encountered the irreducible diamond
In the rock. Yet now it is over. Omniscience is not for man.
Christen me, therefore, that my acts in the dark may be just,
And adapt my partial vision to the limitation of time.'

The Forge of the Solstice

The best are older : with the unrest time brings,
No absolute remains to bind them fast.
One scrawls on rock the names of hallowed things,
Letters and hieroglyphs that yet shall last
When darkness measures with a martyr's eye
The glories shed by life's unchanging tree.

Another, curbing vigour on his page
To movement, makes the abounding life his own
And rhythmic finds in a discordant age,
Singing like living fountains sprung from stone,
Those unifying harmonies of line
Torn from creative nature. Light is born

Under believing fingers. Men refute
By inward protest what their masters teach,
Seeking a deeper meaning. One is mute,
Fearing far more the heresies of speech
Than watchful waiting. Figures move ; they pass
Across the cave. Before them flies heaven's glass,

And out of it now falls the winter sun,
Leaving a ceaseless myth of moving waves,
Till darkness quiets all things. Man is one :
The identity survives its many graves.
First was the hunter, then the prophet ; last,
The artificer, compounding in one ghost

Hunter and prey, prophet and witness, brought
Into that circle where all riddles end.
Love gives their art a body in which thought
Draws, not from time but wisdom, till it bend
The solstice like a bow, and bring time round
White with young stars, quick from the forge
    they have found.

Swedenborg's Skull

Note this survivor, bearing the mark of the violator,
Yet still a vessel of uninterrupted calm.
Its converse is ended. They beat on the door of his coffin,
But they could not shake or destroy that interior psalm
Intended for God alone, for his sole Creator.
For gold they broke into his tomb.

The mark of the pick is upon him, that rough intrusion
Upon the threshold and still place of his soul.
With courtesy he received them. They stopped, astonished,
Where the senses had vanished, to see the dignified skull
Discoursing alone, entertaining those guests of his vision
Whose wit made the axe-edge dull.

Here the brain flashed its fugitive lightning, its secret appraising,
Where marble, settled in utmost composure, appears.
Here the heirs of the heavens were disposed in symmetrical orders
And a flash of perception transfigured the darkness of years.
The mark of a membrane is linked with those traffickers grazing
Its province of princes and spheres.

Where the robbers looked, meditations disputed the legacy
Of the dreaming mind, and the rungs of their commonplace crime
Gave way to swift places of angels, caught up in division
From the man upon earth ; but his patience now played like a mime,
And they could not break down or interpret the skull in its privacy
Or take him away from his time.

So I see it today, the inscrutable mask of conception
Arrested in death. Hard, slender and grey, it transcends
The enquiring senses, even as a shell toiling inward,
Caught up from the waters of change by a traveller who bends
His piercing scrutiny, yields but a surface deception,
Still guarding the peace it defends.

The Tributary Seasons

I can discern at last how grew
This tree, so naked and so true.
'Spring was my death; when all is sung,
It was the Autumn made me young.'

Midwinter: packed with ice the butt,
Splitting its sides.
Roots hard as iron; the back door shut.
Heaped wood a ringing axe divides.
Sacks on the pipes. No river flows,
No tap, no spring. A skater goes
Skimming across the pond. A stone
Stays on the ice where it is thrown.
Under a bone a blue-tit swings,
The keen light glancing on his wings.
To robins crusts and crumbs are tossed,
Yellow against the white of frost.
A quilted world. Glazed mistletoe.
Spades glint, and sledges glide, on snow.
Boys scoop it up with tingling hands,
Steadying the snowman where he stands,
Numb into dusk. Then holly boughs
Darken the walls in many a house,
While moth-flakes pile on wood and ground,
Muffling the panes, and hide all sound.
   The tree of Winter, Winter's tree:
   Winter a dark, a naked tree.

What you have seen you have not known.
Look for it now that Winter's gone.
The Winter stars, the silent king,
The angelic night, give way to Spring.

March into May: the lengthening day
With forward light

Kindles the finches in their play,
Turning their wings in amorous flight.
No star in frost more brightly shines
Than, in white grass, these celandines.
Now sunlight warms and light wind shakes
The unopened blooms. The jonquil breaks
Clean from its sheath. Gold wax and gums
Hold the buds fast. The chestnut comes
First into leaf, its trance-bound hands
Pulled from the shell by silken strands,
Breathless and white. The sap unseen
Climbs the stiff stalk and makes all green.
All timeless coils break through, sublime,
The skins and cerements of time.
What spikenard makes the dark earth sweet?
Life from the hyacinth's winding-sheet
Breathes on the fields, and thrushes sing:
'Earth is our mother. Spring is Spring.'
  The tree of Spring, the selfsame tree:
  Spring is the green, foretelling tree.

What you have seen you cannot know.
Winter is gone, and Spring will go.
These blossoms falling through long grass
Will fade from swallows' quivering glass.

Now the meridian. Summer glows,
A furnace weighed,
Deep in red rose and burnet rose,
Entranced by its own musk and shade.
Birds sing more softly. Foxgloves keep
Over the hedge a misty sleep.
Gardens are secret in their walls
And mountains feel their waterfalls.
Murmuring among thick blooms, the bees
Plunge, and in silence honey seize,
Then bear it droning to their hive
Of light by labour kept alive.

Yet still the toil, where leaves are dense,
Breathes of the Spring's first frankincense.
Butterflies dance in blazing beams.
Great trees are hushed, and still the streams.
On river banks, where boughs serene
Reflect their every shade of green,
Bathers take rest, and bodies come
Naked to peace, and their first home.
    The tree of Summer, Summer's tree,
    Lost in the sleep of Adam's tree.

Might this indeed have been the prime,
That Eden state of lasting time?
Men reap the grain and tend the vine,
Heaping their tributes, bread and wine.

    At last late leaves bright-coloured bring,
    Turning time's keys,
    Those fruits foreshadowed by the Spring.
    Acorns and nuts restore their trees.
    As certain jewels have the power
    To magnetize and guide the hour,
    So seeds before our eyes are strewn
    Fast hidden in the pod's cocoon.
    These die, yet in themselves they keep
    All seasons cradled in their sleep.
    Guarding the lost through calms and storms,
    These are the year's eternal forms,
    An alphabet whose letters all
    Mark out a sacred festival.
    The birth of vision from these urns
    Into whose silence dust returns
    Fills the dense wood. Saint Hubert's rein
    Stops the swift horse; for there again
    A stag between its antlers holds
    Heaven's unique glory, and the world's.
        Tree of beginning, Autumn tree:
        Divine imagination's tree.

Poet and Goldsmith

He was now alone. The lovers had wandered across
The field. About him the air fell sweet with singing.
Very close to his eyes a bird was carrying moss.
It gathered a wisp of straw, pecked, and looked up,
And flew to a secret nest. He watched the bough
Tremble. Now it was still. There was dew on the field.
Petals began to close. The roots of the elms
Held his wonder: 'Be warned: about you are symbols.'

Over sea, gold distance hung in a fiery crucible.
No fingers, however cunning, could sift the grains
Of hurrying sand. Mathematical, yet inscrutable,
Each rose with the rising wave, then slipped through the hour-glass.
No shore could set a term to the curlew's call.
The voice returned to itself round the sevenfold world
And perched on mystery. Night, like a working goldsmith,
Heard waves beat on the indestructible core.

The poet sang: 'All ages bud like the sycamore.
Brown keys spin down to beginning. There are two natures.
Blest are the lost, packed hidden within life's door
Like seeds in the husk. Yet, since a small man climbed
The crooked trunk, and groped, and sat in the branch,
The minutiae of earth are changed, and the blackbird's praises
Are now twofold: they speak, and they speak beyond knowledge.
Even so, these hands have touched the harp of the dead.'

The dying light moved down to birth in his eyes,
And his eyes experienced music. Night was athletic;
A powerful glory tensed the proportioned skies.
And he murmured again: 'One thought that is dear to love:
True characters do not age in each other's eyes.
Indeed, we die each moment the life of another,
And there is no separation, no spear in the side,
Except in that forgetting of mutual death.'

'Unsearchable distance! The gliding avalanche
Wounds me,' he sang. Sycamore leaves against heaven
Moving, sighed. Then, as he touched one branch,
The force of his fingers entered the roots of the tree.
'Earth, cradle of riches; the speed and grace of the hunter,
Born here; plumes of the pheasant shining with dew:
They speak, singly, of inexhaustible treasure.
Night speaks, the artificer, beating out gold.'

Peace in the Welsh Hills

Calm is the landscape when the storm has passed,
Brighter the fields, and fresh with fallen rain.
Where gales beat out new colour from the hills
Rivers fly faster, and upon their banks
Birds preen their wings, and irises revive.
Not so the cities burnt alive with fire
Of man's destruction: when their smoke is spent,
No phoenix rises from the ruined walls.

I ponder now the grief of many rooms.
Was it a dream, that age, when fingers found
A satisfaction sleeping in dumb stone,
When walls were built responding to the touch
In whose high gables, in the lengthening days,
Martins would nest? Though crops, though lives, would fail,
Though friends dispersed, unchanged the walls would stay,
And still those wings return to build in Spring.

Here, where the earth is green, where heaven is true
Opening the windows, touched with earliest dawn,
In the first frost of cool September days,
Chrysanthemum weather, presaging great birth,
Who in his heart could murmur or complain:
'The light we look for is not in this land'?
That light is present, and that distant time
Is always here, continually redeemed.

There is a city we must build with joy
Exactly where the fallen city sleeps.
There is one road through village, town and field,
On whose robust foundation Chaucer dreamed
A ride could wed the opposites in man.
There proud walls may endure, and low walls feed
The imagination if they have a vine
Or shadowy barn made rich with gathered corn.

Great mansions fear from their surrounding trees
The invasion of a wintry desolation
Filling their rooms with leaves. And cottages
Bring the sky down as flickering candles do,
Leaning on their own shadows. I have seen
Vases and polished brass reflect black windows
And draw the ceiling down to their vibrations,
Thick, deep, and white-washed, like a bank of snow.

To live entwined in pastoral loveliness
May rest the eyes, throw pictures on the mind,
But most we need a metaphor of stone
Such as those painters had whose mountain-cities
Cast long, low shadows on the Umbrian hills.
There, in some courtyard on the cobbled stone,
A fountain plays, and through a cherub's mouth
Ages are linked by water in the sunlight.

All of good faith that fountain may recall,
Woman, musician, boy, or else a scholar
Reading a Latin book. They seem distinct,
And yet are one, because tranquillity
Affirms the Judgment. So, in these Welsh hills,
I marvel, waking from a dream of stone,
That such a peace surrounds me, while the city
For which all long has never yet been built.

Bread and the Stars

How clear the stars to-night,
All the bright heaven how still!
Under dense groves of white
This glistening sheet displays
A frost of spellbound streams.
All is at rest. I gaze
Out on the paths and beams
Of night's unresting mill.

So deadly white this frost,
It kills both bird and mouse
Hid where the swedes are tossed
Into an iron barn.
Owls upon vermin feast.
Their solemn hootings warn,
When every sound has ceased,
Man in his mortal house.

Nothing now comes between
The inane and this hard crust
Close to the roots of men
As shrouds are to their dead.
How precious now the loss
Of souls whose printless tread
Where many footprints cross
Takes the whole night on trust.

How full the clustered sky!
Beyond the uncounted crop
Of stars I still descry
Where the white millstream runs
Glittering in ghostly race
New multitudes of suns,
While here galactic space
Hangs, like a frozen drop.

Night with her teeming brood
Unites the faculties
To polarize the blood
Moving, yet fixed and still,
Drawn to her secret North.
The same unerring will
That called conception forth
Now bids the bloodstream freeze.

Yet men to Earth are bound,
To heats from which they grew.
They sift the stars who pound
The corn with leavening yeast
Till the whole bread is made;
And plenty crowns their feast,
Wine from a cellar's shade
Preserving all that's true.

None need look far for proof
That passion bears the sky.
The elect, beneath time's roof
Dropping from steadfast eyes
The plummet of their peace,
Hold to each man that dies
A measure of increase,
A cup to judge life by.

Bread of dear life, and cup
Or glass made dull by breath,
Those spinning worlds far up
Whose fiery swarms recede,
All cannot match the weight
Of your immediate need,
Brought on a man-fired plate
To break his fast to death.

Clear night, great distances,
Faith, like a pestle, drums
Your baffling silences.
Hard though the wintry crust,
What truth has man but loaves?
Bread will compel man's trust,
And not the starry groves:
Wisdom is hid in crumbs.

In the Protestant Cemetery, Rome

Where cypress and acacia stand,
Grave upon grave on either hand,
Touching the wall's peculiar bell
I hear the new vibration tell
I entered through this very door
Violent, yet measured, years before,
To stand in shadow from the sky
Where Shelley and Trelawny lie
And find the spot where sunlight eats
The letters on the grave of Keats.
It was a moment when I still
Knew no remedy for time's ill,
Among the many or the few
No power effective to renew
Substance loved and treasured most,
Seeming irreparably lost.
Watching those animated trees
Move above the contraries,
Writing shadows on the dead,
Lifting the shades, their dying shed,
I, like one who was gagged and bound,
Having no words but in the ground,
Defying time and memory,
Sought to resolve their tragedy.

Nothing has changed. No string has gone
This morning from the harp of stone
Above the epitaph which belies
That youth who looked with earnest eyes,
Confident that he would be
Remembered by posterity.
Yet what a monument for tears!
Severn, surviving sixty years
That long day on which he penned
The portrait of his dying friend,

Is laid in death beside him now
Underneath the selfsame bough.
Keats, whose searing, fevered ache
Boyhood's ambition could not slake,
Found that his friend's devotion brought
Anodyne for the pain of thought.
Blossoms falling through the air
Make the very dust aware
By what sad stages he had come,
Leaving great hopes, to die in Rome.
There hangs a darkness, as of waves,
On Shelley's and Trelawny's graves.
The sailor who outlived his friend
Like Severn Keats, and in the end
Moored his boat beside that stone,
Neighbours him now, as time moves on.
In Shelley's coat when he was drowned
Keats' book, with Aeschylus', was found.
He, so unlike Keats, for whom
He brought his poem to the tomb,
Well understood what gifts were hid
Here, by Cestius' pyramid.
He knew *Hyperion*, knew his pall,
But did not know the unfinished *Fall*.
Shelley, who from the first began
His concept of a sinless man,
Inspired by passion's desperate stream
Translating substance into dream,
Yet who transfigured him to thought,
Making of life what it is not,
Ignored that resurrection must
Come of true substance, and of dust.
Byron to his burial came
And saw Trelawny through the flame
Pluck the heart which would not burn
Destined to this unspeaking urn,
When on the funeral pyre he lay,
Carried from Lerici Bay.

How still the graveyard : one at peace
And one so restless. Time must cease
Before they understand each other.
Yet now they do, for now their mother
Casts on them her falling leaves.
No longer the miraculous grieves
For youth cut off, reclaimed by age,
Where history sets a tragic stage.
Character keeps its vesture on
Holding the body, though it's gone;
And the paired friends, a space apart,
Draw the leaves' whisperings, heart to heart.
Yet now once more the gate is closed,
The new life seized, the limbs disposed.
Altered by a gentle breeze,
The cypress and acacia trees
Take root again where first they grew,
The place where contraries are true.

Loiterers

This my birthplace? No, friend, this is Xanion's,
He, the owner of that yellow barley.
Mischievous chicory was all I planted:
Blue-eyed, we played here.

O, could the mayfly of memory wing back
Through bee-bustle and waspish digressions,
Certainly here it would find us standing,
Left in this cart-rut.

There the house glinted, near the tilting hay-rick,
Down through rose-ramblers to the prosperous earth-mould.
There the sky flashed to the windows, and the windows
Flashed to our young eyes.

Dawn's early singers, missel-thrush and skylark,
Still mark the track we followed to the cornfield.
Foxgloves in midge-light hid the turning river
Swept by the swallows.

Fallen is the house to the earth-mould, fallen.
Quick, for we lag here. If the dust is pollen
Robbed by the butterfly, stolen by the mayfly,
Why should we sigh, then?

A True Picture Restored

Nearer the pulse than other themes
His deathborn claims are pressed.
Fired first by Milton, then the dreams
Of Herbert's holy breast,
Out of his days the sunlight streams
And fills the burning West.

I look where soon the frosty Plough
Shall hang above the sill
And see the colours westward flow
To green Carmarthen's hill.
There sinks the sky of changes now
On waters never still.

Praise God, although a time is gone
That shall not come again,
If ever morning rightly shone,
A glass to make all plain,
The man I mourn can make it live,
Every fallen grain.

I see the house where we would meet;
I see my steps return,
Kicking the sparks of the Swansea street,
And still those windows burn,
Struck by the sunrise hour of life
With all men's lives to learn.

My echoing footsteps when they stop
Reconstitute the town,
That working window at the top,
The neophyte and clown
Setting the reel and arc-light up
To pull illusion down.

The various roofs beneath that house,
The crooked roads and straight,
The excess or strictness God allows
In every devious fate,
He honoured these with early vows
And cursed the aloof with late.

The latest dead, the latest dead,
How should he have died,
He in whom Eden's morning
Had left its ancient pride,
Adam, God, and maiden,
Love, and the yearning side?

And Wales, when shall you have again
One so true as he,
Whose hand was on the mountain's heart,
The rising of the sea,
And every praising bird that cries
Above the estuary?

He never let proud nature fall
Out of its pristine state.
The hunchback fed upon a love
That made the crooked straight,
No single promise broken
On which the heart must wait.

The heron poised above the glass
With straight and stabbing bill,
Among the water's moods that pass
Choosing to strike and kill,
Transfixed the sky with holiest eye
When the whole heart was still.

Down to the solstice moves the sun
And through Saint Lucie's night
Under the earth all rivers run

Back to the birth of light.
Among the living he was one
Who felt the world in flight.

Climbing Cwmdonkin's dock-based hill,
I found his lamp-lit room,
The great light in the forehead
Watching the waters' loom,
Compiling there his doomsday book
Or dictionary of doom.

More times than I can call to mind
I heard him reading there.
His eyes with fervour could make blind
All clocks about a stair
On which the assenting foot divined
The void and clustered air.

That was the centre of the world,
That was the hub of time.
The complex vision faded now,
The simple grew sublime.
There seemed no other valid stair
For wondering feet to climb.

That strictest, lie-disrobing act
Testing the poem read
Which, after toil and plumbing,
Left the first cause unsaid,
Showed me his nature then as now,
The life he gave the dead.

There, near Cwmdonkin, first and last,
Witness of lives below,
He held the unrisen wisdom fast
From heaven in overthrow,
Where lamps of hooded meaning cast
Light on the words below.

And later, in that toppling house
Over the village hearse,
Where the Portreeve assembled
His birds and characters,
It was the dying earth he gave
To heaven in living verse.

In London, when the blinds were drawn
Blackening a barbarous sky,
He plucked, beneath the accusing beams,
The mote out of his eye.
In the one death his eye discerned
The death all deaths must die.

'My immortality,' he said,
'Now matters to my soul
Less than the deaths of others.'
And would not fame enrol
Every forgotten character
If Shakespeare held the scroll?

The latest dead, the latest dead,
What power could pull him down
Who on a breath of vision
Could animate a town,
Could plunder every shy retreat
And give the lost renown?

Not by the wars of human minds
Nor by the jealous word
Nor by the black of London's blinds
Or coffin's rattling cord,
But by the stillness of that voice
The picture is restored.

Let each whose soul is in one place
Still to that place be true.
The man I mourn could honour such

With every breath he drew.
I never heard him wish to take
A life from where it grew.

And yet the man I mourn is gone,
He who could give the rest
So much to live for till the grave,
And do it all in jest.
Hard it must be, beyond this day,
For even the grass to rest.

Vine

Deep-rooted vine, delay your fruit
Beyond youth's rashness. I have seen
Rich promise wither to the root
Before its time had been.

Drain all the darkness of the soil
And stand there shrivelled, crisp and dry,
Too lifeless in your parchment coil
To open one green eye.

Some watch the March winds animate
Those early bulbs in Winter's bed.
Envy them not, but keep your state.
Let others think you dead.

Contain in secrecy that balm
Strengthening the sap before it move,
That the broad leaves from wells of calm
One day grow dark with love.

I know a tree as dry as yours.
The patient leaf is put forth late.
Its life is anchored in the hours
For which the heart must wait.

Good Friday

After the winter solstice came
Ice and low flame,
The cockerel step by which the light
Shortened the sleep of earth and night.

And slowly as the days of Lent
Waxed and were spent,
Trees, birds and flowers all increased
In expectation of the feast.

Spring with such promise did abound
That the gemmed ground
Already showed in clustered grass
The printless light of unseen stars.

But now light grows where rays decline.
Now the crushed wine
Transfigures all, leaf, blossom, fruit,
By reference to the sacred root.

Day must die here that day may break.
Time must forsake
Time, and this moment be preferred
To any copy, light or word.

In this a night we apprehend
Which has no end.
Day dies. We make our choice, and say:
'This, this we seek ; no second day.'

Not in the speculative skies
Instruction lies,
But in the nails of darkness driven
Into these hands which hold up heaven.

For, as old ages antedate
Love's present weight,
So the pulse falling gives the chain
Momentum to what years remain.

All lives, to flourish, here should stop
Still; and all hope
To live, must die here first, and pull
New ages to this mountain skull.

Now let the geography of lands
Learn from these hands,
And from these feet the unresting seas
Take, from unfathomed grief, their ease.

Our mortal life is composite
Until we knit
All possible days to this, and make
A seal, from which true day must break.

Come, Easter, come: I was afraid
Your star had strayed.
It was behind our darkest fears
Which could not see their God for tears.

Great Nights Returning

Great nights returning, midnight's constellations
Gather from groundfrost that unnatural brilliance.
Night now transfigures, walking in the starred ways,
Tears for the living.

Earth now takes back the secret of her changes.
All the wood's dropped leaves listen to your footfall.
Night has no tears, no sound among the branches;
Stopped is the swift stream.

Spirits were joined when hazel leaves were falling.
Then the stream hurrying told of separation.
This is the fires' world, and the voice of Autumn
Stilled by the death-wand.

Under your heels the icy breath of Winter
Hardens all roots. The Leonids are flying.
Now the crisp stars, the circle of beginning;
Death, birth, united.

Nothing declines here. Energy is fire-born.
Twigs catch like stars or serve for your divining.
Lean down and hear the subterranean water
Crossed by the quick dead.

Now the soul knows the fire that first composed it
Sinks not with time but is renewed hereafter.
Death cannot steal the light which love has kindled
Nor the years change it.